Book/Online Audio

SCHIRMER'S LIBRARY
OF MUSICAL CLASSICS

Vol. 1767-B

Georg Philipp T

Four Sonatas
For Flute and Piano

To access companion recorded accompaniments online, visit:
www.halleonard.com/mylibrary

Enter Code
2245-0352-7809-7214

Edited by Milton Wittgenstein
Figured Bass Realization by Thomas Wilt

On the accompaniment recordings:
JEANNIE YU

ISBN 978-1-4584-6563-4

G. SCHIRMER, Inc.

DISTRIBUTED BY
HAL•LEONARD®
7777 W. BLUEMOUND RD. P.O. BOX 13819 MILWAUKEE, WI 53213

www.schirmer.com
www.halleonard.com

CONTENTS

Sonata in G Major

3	Cantabile
4	Allegro
7	Affettuoso
8	Allegro

Sonata in C minor

13	Allegro
15	Adagio
16	Allegro assai
19	Ondeggiando, ma non adagio
21	Allegro

Sonata in F Major

25	Vivace
27	Largo
28	Allegro

Sonata in B-flat Major

31	Largo
34	Allegro
36	Allegretto
37	Vivace
41	Allegro

Pianist on the recordings: Jeannie Yu

The price of this publication includes access to companion recorded accompaniments online, for download or streaming, using the unique code found on the title page.
Visit **www.halleonard.com/mylibrary** and enter the access code.

Sonata in G Major

Georg Philipp Telemann
(1681–1767)

4

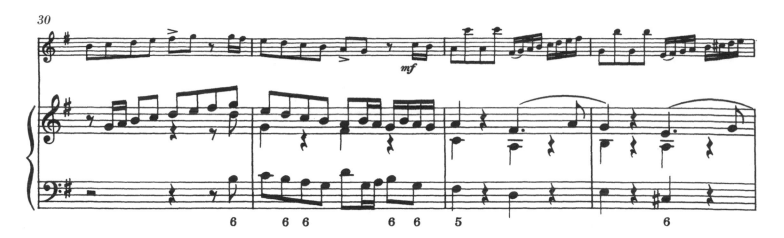

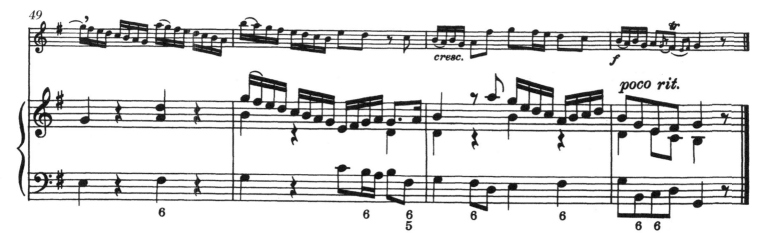

Allegro ♩ = 138

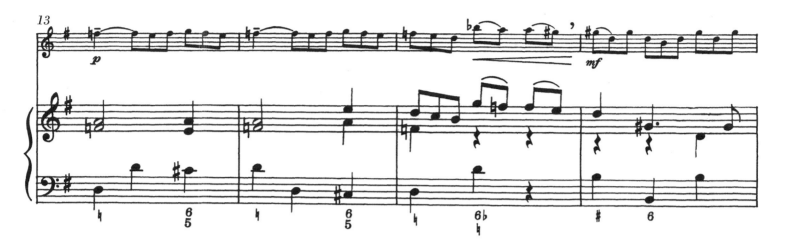

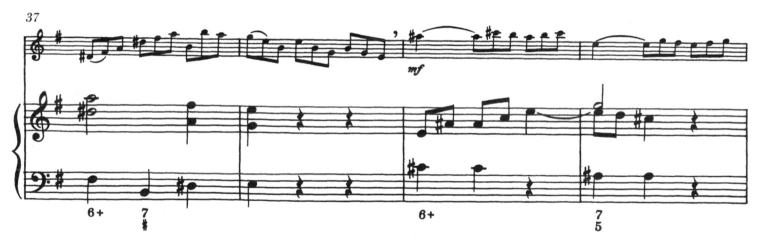

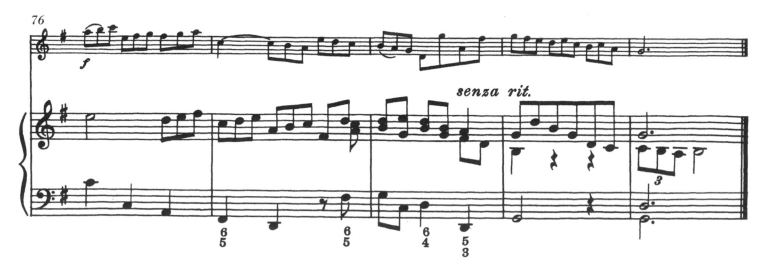

Sonata in C minor
from the *Methodischen Sonaten* (1732)

Georg Philipp Telemann
(1681–1767)

Allegro assai ♩ = 100

18

Ondeggiando, ma non adagio ♩=44

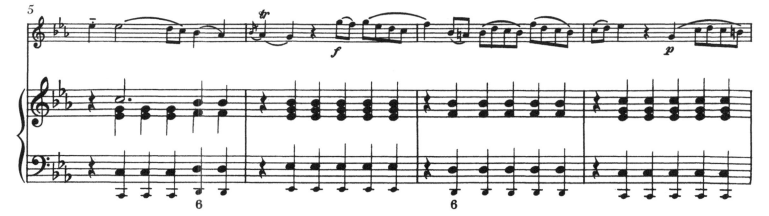

Vol. 1767-B

Georg Philipp Telemann

Four Sonatas
For Flute and Piano

Edited by Milton Wittgenstein
Figured Bass Realization by Thomas Wilt

On the accompaniment recordings:
JEANNIE YU

ISBN 978-1-4584-6563-4

G. SCHIRMER, Inc.

DISTRIBUTED BY

HAL•LEONARD®

7777 W. BLUEMOUND RD. P.O. BOX 13819 MILWAUKEE, WI 53213

www.schirmer.com
www.halleonard.com

CONTENTS

Sonata in G Major

2	Cantabile
2	Allegro
4	Affettuoso
4	Allegro

Sonata in C minor

6	Allegro
6	Adagio
7	Allegro assai
8	Ondeggiando, ma non adagio
9	Allegro

Sonata in F Major

10	Vivace
11	Largo
11	Allegro

Sonata in B-flat Major

12	Largo
13	Allegro
14	Allegretto
14	Vivace
15	Allegro

Pianist on the recordings: Jeannie Yu

Sonata in G Major

Georg Philipp Telemann
(1681–1767)

The pianist plays the following as an introduction on the accompaniment track:

The pianist plays measure 52 as an introduction on the accompaniment track.

Affettuoso ♪= 76

The pianist plays measure 2 as an introduction on the accompaniment track.

Allegro ♩= 138

The pianist plays measure 2 as an introduction on the accompaniment track.

Sonata in C minor

from the *Methodischen Sonaten* (1732)

Georg Philipp Telemann
(1681–1767)

The pianist plays measures 48–50 as an introduction on the accompaniment track.

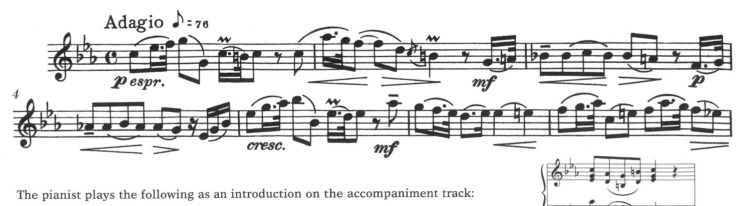

The pianist plays the following as an introduction on the accompaniment track:

Allegro assai ♩=100

The pianist plays measure 41 as an introduction on the accompaniment track.

8

Ondeggiando, ma non adagio ♩ = 44

mf dolce

The pianist plays the following as an introduction on the accompaniment track:

The pianist plays measures 63–64 as an introduction on the accompaniment track.

Sonata in F Major
from *Der Getreue Musikmeister* (1728)

Georg Philipp Telemann
(1681–1767)

The pianist plays measures 31–32 as an introduction on the accompaniment track.

The pianist plays measures 15–16 as an introduction on the accompaniment track.

The pianist plays measures 45–46 as an introduction on the accompaniment track.

Sonata in B-flat Major

from the *Methodischen Sonaten* (1732)

Georg Philipp Telemann
(1681–1767)

The pianist plays the following as an introduction on the accompaniment track:

Allegro ♩=120

The pianist plays measures 54–56 as an introduction on the accompaniment track.

14

The pianist plays measures 41–42 as an introduction on the accompaniment track.

The pianist plays measures 50–51 as an introduction on the accompaniment track.

The pianist plays measure 16 as an introduction on the accompaniment track.

29

32

Allegro ♩.=112

5

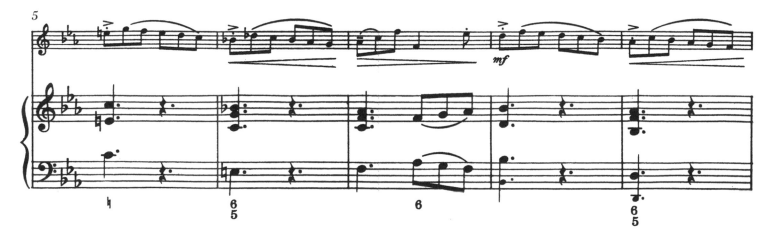

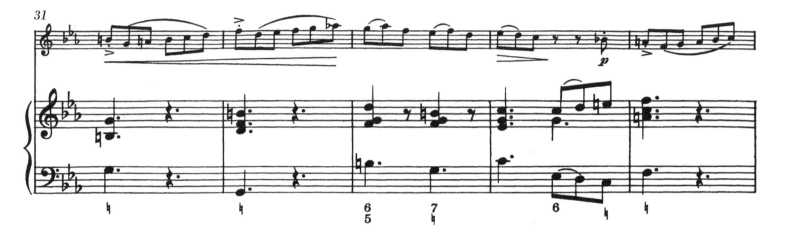

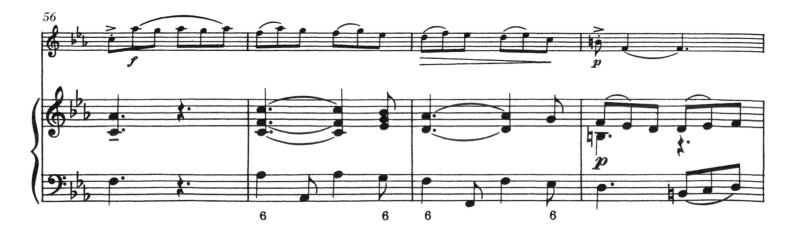

Sonata in F Major
from *Der Getreue Musikmeister* (1728)

Georg Philipp Telemann
(1681–1767)

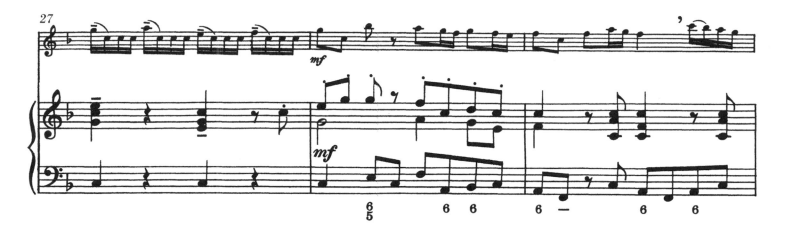

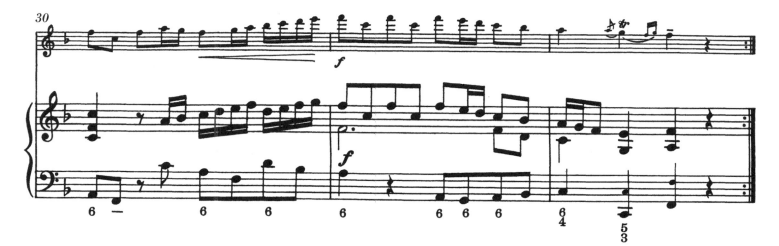

★ The lower octave of the bass may be added throughout this movement.

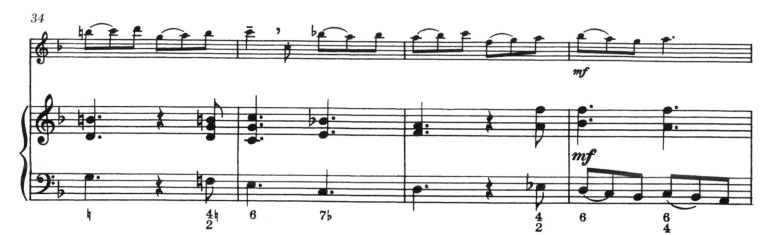

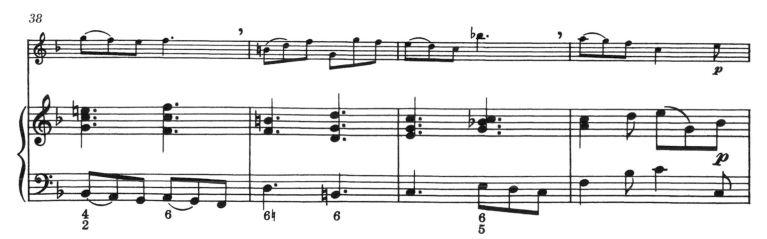

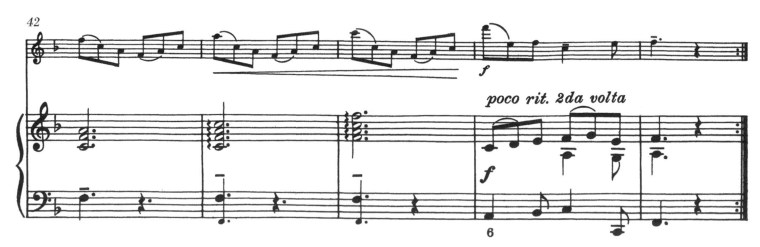

Sonata in B-flat Major
from the *Methodischen Sonaten* (1732)

Georg Philipp Telemann
(1681–1767)

32

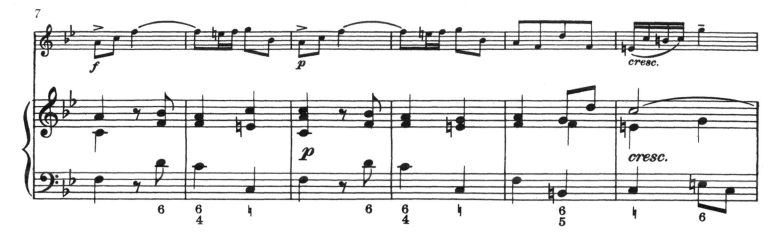

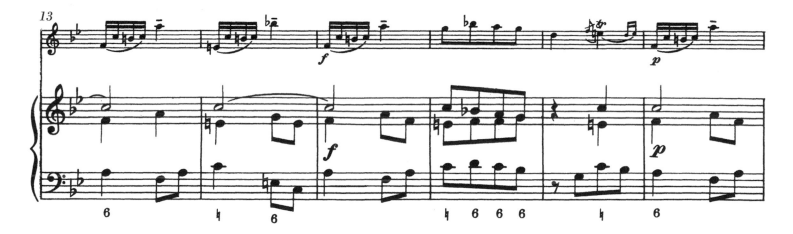

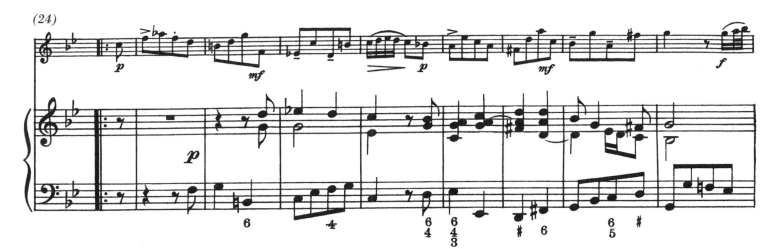

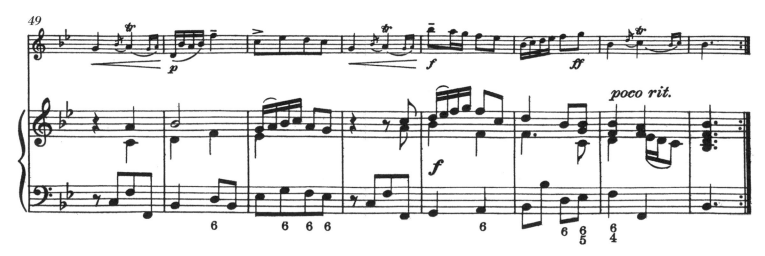

Allegretto ♪=120

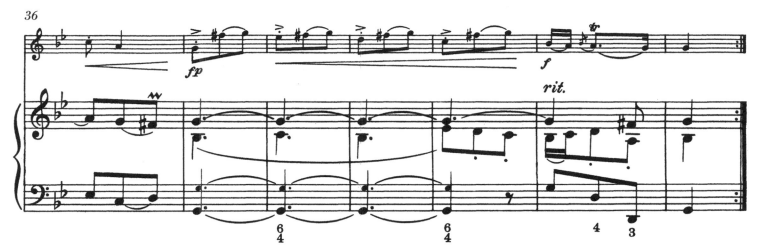

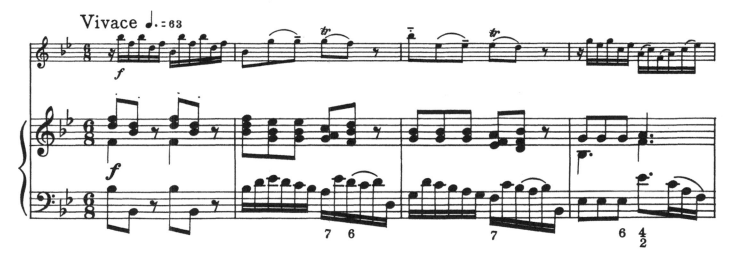

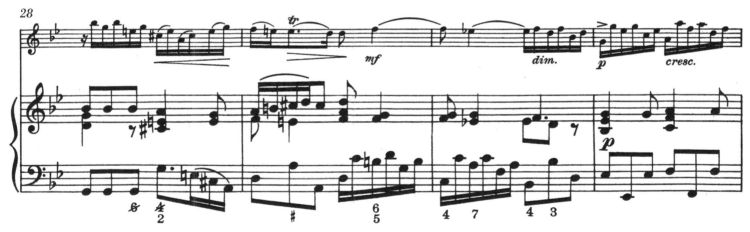

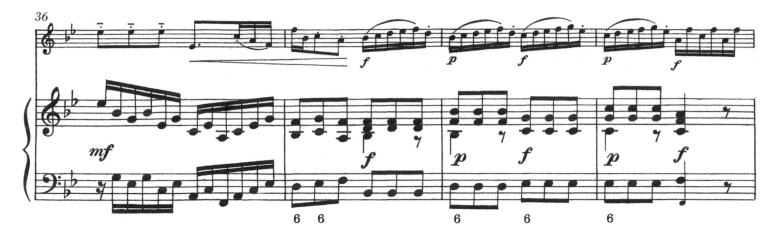

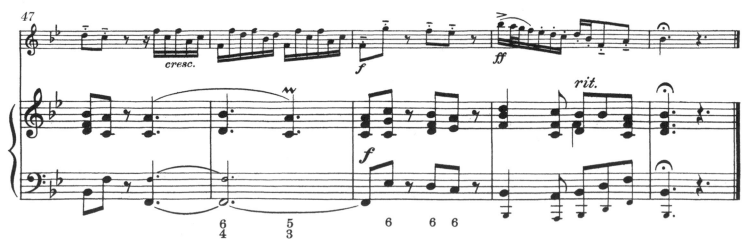